D0100693

ON ASSIGNMENT

Learning about
Ocean
Animals

Rebecca L. Johnson

PICTURE CREDITS
Cover (background and back inset), pages 20–21 Corbis; cover (left inset), 5 (background), 15 Michael Heithaus/National Geographic Society; cover (right inset), pages 4 (inset), 6–7, 20, 26, 30 Birgit Buhleier; page 1 Charles O'Rear/Corbis; pages 2–3, 6 (inset), 12–13 James Watt/Animals Animals; pages 3, 8–9 (bottom), 10 (top), 14, 16 (bottom), 22, 23 (left), 23 (right), 24 (inset) Greg Marshall; pages 4–5, 18–19 Bob Cranston/Animals Animals; pages 8–9 (top) Nick Caloyianis; page 10 (bottom) Joel Sartore/NGS Image Collection; page 11 Mehdi Bakhtiari/National Geographic Society; page 13 National Geographic Television and Film; page 17 (bottom) Greg Marshall, photographed by Mark Thiessen; page 24–25 (top) McDonald Wildlife Photography/Animals Animals.

ARTWORK
Linda Kelen

Produced through the worldwide resources of the National Geographic Society, John M. Fahey, Jr., President and Chief Executive Officer; Gilbert M. Grosvenor, Chairman of the Board; Nina D. Hoffman, Executive Vice President and President, Books and Education Publishing Group.

PREPARED BY NATIONAL GEOGRAPHIC SCHOOL PUBLISHING
Ericka Markman, Senior Vice President and President Children's Books and Education Publishing Group; Steve Mico, Senior Vice President, Publisher; Marianne Hiland, Executive Editor; Jim Hiscott, Design Manager; Kristin Hanneman, Illustrations Manager; Matt Wascavage, Manager of Publishing Services; Sean Philpotts, Production Manager.

MANUFACTURING AND QUALITY MANAGEMENT
Christopher A. Liedel, Chief Financial Officer; Phillip L. Schlosser, Director; Clifton M. Brown III, Manager.

PROGRAM DEVELOPMENT
Kate Boehm Jerome

CONSULTANTS/REVIEWERS
Dr. James Shymansky, E. Desmond Lee Professor of Science Education, University of Missouri-St. Louis
Glen Phelan, science writer, Palatine, Illinois

BOOK DEVELOPMENT
Thomas Nieman, Inc.

BOOK DESIGN
Herman Adler Design

Published by the National Geographic Society
1145 17th Street, N.W.
Washington, D.C. 20036-4688

ISBN: 978-0-7922-8446-8

Eighth Printing 2018
Printed in USA.

A humpback whale slips beneath the water's surface.

Contents

An Antarctic penguin takes a swim with a special camera on its back.

Greg Marshall

Introduction

Hitching a Ride

Brightly colored fish swirled around Greg Marshall as he glided over the reef. He checked his air supply. It was almost time to end the dive. Then he saw the shark. It was swimming right toward him. The shark came closer, and closer. . . .

Greg held his breath as the shark swam past. That's when he saw the **remora** on the shark. A remora is a long, skinny fish. With a suction-cup-like structure on its head, it can attach to other fish.

After the dive, Greg could not stop thinking about what he had seen. He wondered if a camera could be stuck to a shark, like a remora. If he could figure out how to do that—and get the camera back—he'd see the ocean from the shark's point of view. The "hitchhiking" camera would go where the shark went. It would record what the shark saw and did.

Greg's idea became an invention called Crittercam. In this book you'll go on assignment to meet the Crittercam team. You'll learn how Crittercam shows us the secret lives of ocean animals.

A remora hitches a ride on a shark.

Creating Crittercam

A whale breaks the water's surface. Then it arches through the air and disappears below. What does it do after it dives out of sight?

Humpback whales

That's a good question, and one scientists have tried to answer for years. Studying animals like whales, sharks, and seals isn't easy. They can dive deeper than divers in scuba gear. They can swim faster than small submarines can travel. Scuba divers and subs can also scare ocean animals and make them act in unnatural ways.

With a flip of its tail, a whale takes a dive.

That's why Greg liked the idea of attaching cameras to sea creatures. It would be a way to swim with them without scaring them.

In 1987, Greg started building Crittercam. He began by taking apart a video camcorder. Bit by bit, he took out all the parts he didn't need. He got down to the camera's basic parts. He placed those parts in a waterproof metal tube.

The tube was **streamlined** so that water would flow smoothly around it. The more streamlined Crittercam was, the less **drag** it would create for the animal wearing it. Imagine how hard it would be to swim wearing a backpack. That's drag!

The tube had to be strong, too. It would probably get bumped as an animal wearing it searched for food.

7

Crittercam on a turtle

First Tests

Greg put everything together and made the first **prototype**, or test model, of Crittercam. It looked like a toy rocket with little fins on the sides.

Then Crittercam had to be tested. Some tests were pretty simple. Greg plunged the prototype into a full bathtub to test it for leaks. He made sure that it was **buoyant**. The camera would have to float. After all, once the camera was done taking pictures, Greg had to get it back.

The camera couldn't be too buoyant. If it was, it would make the animal wearing it rise in the water. Crittercam had to be like a remora—streamlined and nearly weightless underwater.

The next step was to test the prototype on an animal. What kind of animal? Something small and easy to handle . . . probably not a shark! Greg chose a captive turtle in Central America.

Changes in Crittercam design, 1987–2000

1987

1988

Greg carefully strapped Crittercam onto the turtle's shell. As the turtle slid into the water of its tank, Greg watched closely. What would the turtle do?

To Greg's relief, the turtle swam around, dived down, and bobbed up to the surface. It didn't pay any attention to the camera on its back. The first big challenge was overcome.

With help from Birgit Buhleier, a biologist friend, Greg kept improving Crittercam. In 1989, they tested it on wild turtles in the Caribbean Sea.

Greg made **harnesses,** or special straps, to hold Crittercam in place on the turtles' shells. He put the harnesses on when the turtles came ashore to lay eggs. At first, the harnesses didn't work. Underwater, the turtles slipped out of them. Greg lost eight Crittercams before he made a harness that worked.

The first fish to wear Crittercam was a captive nurse shark. Watching the shark swim around its tank, Greg could tell that the camera was causing too much drag. So it was back to the drawing board. Every time it was rebuilt, Crittercam got smaller, sleeker, and better.

1991   1994   1997   2000

The Crittercam team safely harnessed the camera to a hippo.

Greg attached a Crittercam to a furry sea lion with glue. The glue will be shed when the animal molts.

What Goes On . . .

A few years later, Greg went to work for National Geographic. Other people joined him to study ocean animals using Crittercam. The Crittercam team experimented with everything from walruses to whales. Each time, the team learned something new.

One goal was to attach Crittercam in ways that are safe for each animal. For example, at first the team attached Crittercam to a shark by poking metal tags into its skin. Later, the team used a clamp. The clamp held the camera on the shark's top fin. No poking was needed.

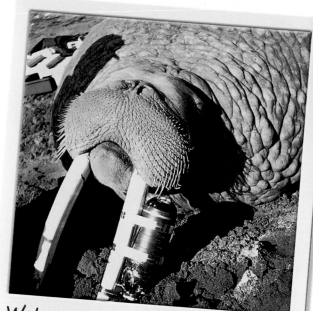

Walruses dig for food in the sea floor. The team clamped Crittercam to a walrus's tusk to learn more.

. . . Must Come Off

The team has also found creative ways to get the cameras off of animals once the videotaping is over.

Some animals, like penguins, hop onto ice or land to rest. When they do, people unclip their harnesses to get the cameras.

Seals and sea lions often come out of the sea to sun themselves. The Crittercams glued to their fur can be easily removed. What if traces of glue are left behind? They'll disappear when the animals go through a **molt**. That's when they naturally shed their fur and grow a brand new coat.

The team has also made a **tether**, or rope, out of a thin strip of metal that dissolves. The tether can tie a camera to an animal. When the tether dissolves, Crittercam pops free.

From the very beginning, Greg Marshall hoped Crittercam would help scientists learn about ocean animals in a new way. And it certainly has!

Way Under the Waves

Open jaws of a great white shark

Imagine for a moment that you want to study the underwater habits of a great white shark. There's a problem. The shark is five times longer than you are tall. And it's got a mouth packed full of some very scary teeth.

Crittercam is tethered to the shark's top, or dorsal, fin.

How would you get Crittercam on—and off—that shark? That's what the Crittercam team had to figure out. Off the coast of South Africa, they used bait to attract great white sharks to the boat. When a shark came close enough, a team member used a long pole to attach a metal tag into its fin. Attached to the tag by a tether was Crittercam. The shark hardly seemed to notice. With a flick of its tail, it swam away. As the shark disappeared, the camera inside Crittercam went to work.

About the time the camera ran out of tape, the tether dissolved. Crittercam floated to the surface, where it sent out a radio signal. The team followed the signal to its source. Soon Crittercam was back on board.

The videotape was worth all the effort. As the tape rolled, the shark's world came into view. The shark's head moved slowly from side to side. Back and forth, back and forth. . . . It took a while for everyone to realize what the shark was doing. It was hunting.

Exactly *how* the shark was hunting was an important discovery. It was looking for silhouettes, or outlines, on the surface of the ocean.

Silhouettes of what, you ask? They could be of a seal, a big fish, or even a person—anything swimming near the surface. When a great white shark spots a shape, it streaks up to attack.

The shark is not injured
as Crittercam is attached.

Tigers in the Sea

The ocean off western Australia is full of sharks, including tiger sharks. Tiger sharks are large and fierce. They eat mostly big fish. But they will eat seals and people, too. Tiger sharks even bite small boats!

The Crittercam team worked with Australian shark scientists for three years. They put Crittercams on more than 40 different tiger sharks.

The videos showed that tiger sharks spend a lot more time in shallow water than people thought. Some of the sharks' favorite spots to hang out are sea-grass beds.

It also turns out that tiger sharks "bounce." They swim up to the surface and then down to the sea floor, like a slowly bouncing ball. Shark experts had never seen this before. They think it may be a way for the sharks to improve their chances of finding food.

Fun Facts!

What's in a Name

Have you ever seen a tiger? The big striped cat is a fierce hunter. Its stripes help it hide in tall grass. Tiger sharks get their name from the fact that they have stripes along their bodies, like the stripes of tigers. The stripes make the sharks harder to see in the sea-grass beds where they often hide.

A tiger shark cruises slowly through a sea-grass bed.

One way to attach Crittercam to a whale is by lowering it onto the animal with a pole.

Sperm Whales

Sperm whales, like other whales, come to the surface to breathe. However, they dive very deep. They travel hundreds of meters below the surface in search of food. They go where there is darkness, cold, and crushing pressure.

The Crittercam team sent more than a camera with each whale. The team added a recorder that could tape any sounds the whale made. They also attached a detector that could track how deep the whale dived and how fast it traveled.

Getting close enough to attach Crittercam to a whale can be very tricky!

A whale has slippery skin. It moves very quickly. Attaching a camera with glue, a clamp, a harness, or a tether would not work. The team decided to attach Crittercam to whales with giant suction cups.

Cool Fix!

The suction cup attached to Crittercam has a vacuum pump. When the pump is turned on, it forces air out of the suction cup. This creates a vacuum. In seconds, the suction cup sucks down tightly onto the whale's skin. When it's time to bring a whale's Crittercam to the surface, the vacuum seal is loosened remotely, with the flip of a switch on a remote control. The suction cup lets go. Soon, Crittercam is bobbing on the waves.

Suction cup

The Crittercam team worked with sperm whale experts. They attached their instruments to sperm whales in the Gulf of Mexico and near islands called the Azores in the Atlantic Ocean.

What did the whale studies show? Sperm whales talk to each other. They use clicks, high-pitched squeals, whistles, and deep "huffing" sounds to communicate. They also give each other "body rubs." They bump into each other, hard enough to make pieces of loose skin peel away. Some experts think this may be how sperm whales **groom** each other.

When Greg Marshall invented Crittercam, some scientists thought it wouldn't work. Others worried that it might even harm ocean animals. But the Crittercam team has proved that hitchhiking cameras are safe. And we've learned a lot about whales and other ocean animals along the way.

 Sperm whales dive to places so deep that there is no light. How do you take video in total darkness? Team members put a ring of tiny "headlights" around the front of Crittercam. The headlights give off near-infrared light. This type of light makes it possible to take pictures in very dark places. Better yet, the light is probably invisible to sperm whales. It doesn't scare them.

Just like Crittercam, remoras
ride along with a sperm whale.

In and Out of the Water

Hawaiian monk seals are easy to study when they're out of the water. With Crittercam, scientists get to ride with the animals into the water. There, the camera has helped people make what could be a life-saving discovery.

Crittercam on a monk seal

A monk seal rests on the sandy shore of a Hawaiian island.

Hawaiian monk seals are **endangered**. Only 1200 to 1300 remain in the wild. Monk seals spend most of their time in shallow water around coral reefs. Laws set aside these shallow reef zones as protected **habitats** for the seals. Even so, the number of monk seals keeps shrinking.

Scientists thought that since monk seals spend so much time in shallow water, that's where they catch most of their food. The Crittercam films showed that this is not true.

Instead of feeding in shallow water, the seals head into deeper water. There they hunt for octopus, crab, eel, and big fish.

Because of Crittercam, scientists now know that the deep water is as important to monk seals as the shallow zones. Crittercam may help scientists get protection for the seals in their deep water habitat, too.

Crittercam tags along with an Emperor penguin.

Penguin wearing Crittercam backward

A penguin streaks up toward the ice.

Diving for Dinner

In Antarctica's bitter cold, scientists study Earth's largest penguins. Emperor penguins can stand more than a meter (3 feet) tall and can weigh as much as 40 kg (about 90 pounds).

The Crittercam team worked with penguin scientists in Antarctica. The group rigged up Emperors with Crittercams. Each penguin wore a harness that held a Crittercam in place on its back. When the birds were all suited up, they dove into the sea through holes in the ice.

The scientists already knew that Emperors make "yo-yo" dives when they search for food. They dive down for several dozen meters, zoom up near the surface, zoom down and up a few more times, and then surface for air.

No one knew where the penguins were catching the fish they ate. Was it down deep, up near the surface, or somewhere in between? Crittercam answered that question.

It turns out that the penguins dive down and then turn to look up. They look at the bottom of the ice overhead. Against the bright white of the ice they can easily spot their favorite fish. So up they go to grab a meal. Then it's down again for another look iceward and then up again for more fish. After a few more yo-yo trips, the penguins pop out of the water with bulging stomachs.

The Crittercam team strapped cameras backward on some penguins. Why? So they could find out what was happening *behind* the penguins. Scientists had wondered if penguins fish on their own or in a group. Results: In these waters, penguins fish alone.

What's Next?

Crittercam lets us follow ocean animals. What about animals that live on land or fly through the air? As it turns out, the Crittercam team is working on that idea right now . . . .

The team started thinking about using Crittercam on land. The biggest problem is weight. In the ocean, Crittercam is buoyed up by the water and becomes almost weightless. Out of the water, every ounce counts.

As video cameras become smaller, Crittercam on land may become a reality. Someday scientists may watch videos taken by tiny cameras strapped to African elephants, wild dogs, or grizzly bears. They might even take flight with an eagle or soar through the night with a bat!

The possibilities are endless. Both in and out of the water, countless animals might let us hitch a ride through their world— with Crittercam.

Birgit Buhleier is one of the scientists working on new ways to use Crittercam.

Bald eagle

Meerkats

Fruit bat

Inventing to Solve a Problem

People are always trying to make life better. Sometimes they find that they need something that just doesn't exist. So they invent it.

Some inventions make life easier. Take the microwave oven. This handy device lets you cook a tasty meal in minutes. Other inventions help people discover new things. People invented telescopes, for example, to learn more about the stars.

Greg Marshall invented Crittercam to learn more about ocean animals. But it didn't happen overnight. Like many inventions, it took a long time to get Crittercam right. But when Greg got all the "kinks" worked out, he had a unique tool for learning more about life in the deep sea.

When you invent, you create something brand new. An invention can solve a problem, or it can meet a certain need. Let's look more closely at what it takes to invent something.

Greg Marshall works on Crittercam.

Step 1   Identify the Need

Need is the driving force behind inventing. When people needed lights to help them see in the dark, they invented candles. Then came the light bulb, followed by the flashlight. The first step in inventing is to identify the need.

The Soda Can Challenge

Imagine that bicycling is something you love to do. And drinking a soda while you're riding makes the experience perfect. The problem? Your bike has a water bottle holder on the frame beneath the seat. But that holder doesn't hold a can of soda very well. Because the holder sits at an angle, soda spills out of the can.

What you really need is a soda can holder on the handlebars. That would keep a can of soda upright and within easy reach. You've never seen a soda can holder like that in a bike shop. Guess you'll just have to invent one!

Step 2   Brainstorm Possible Solutions

What's needed next? Brainpower! Think creatively. Brainstorm possible solutions that will meet the need. Sometimes a great idea comes in a flash. But more often, it takes time and lots of mental energy.

How Can I Carry a Soda Can on My Bike?

You study the handlebars on your bike. Hmm. . . . You need something like your water bottle holder. But it needs to be smaller and stubbier. It could be made out of wire. . . . It has to attach to the handlebars somehow. . . .

You get paper and a pencil and start to sketch what the soda can holder might look like. After a few minutes you come up with a design that you think could work. It's made with things you know you can find around your house.

Step 3 | Build a Prototype

The third step in inventing is to build a prototype. Think of a prototype as a test model of an invention. Building a prototype makes an idea real. It also makes problems easier to spot.

A Soda Can Holder Takes Shape

You rummage around the house and find what you need. You collect some sturdy wire, wire cutters, pliers, and the bottom half of a plastic soda bottle. You cut the wire and bend it around the bottom of the plastic bottle. Then you twist the ends of the wire onto the handlebars.

Step 4 | Test and Revise

The final step in inventing is to test and revise. That is, the invention is tested and then minor changes are made to "fine tune" it. But expect to revise and test many times. You don't often get it right the first time.

I Did It!

You slip a soda into your new holder. Whoops! The weight of the full can makes the holder slip on the handlebars. The soda spills out. You ponder this new problem. Just twisting the wire around the handlebars isn't enough. You need to create a tighter grip. What about duct tape?

You find a roll of tape. You use a few strips of tape to strap the wire firmly onto the handlebars. Then, you test the holder with the can again. This time it stays in place! Pat yourself on the back—you've just invented your own bike-handlebar-soda-can holder!

Problem Solving on Your Own

Understand the Problem

Imagine you've got a big dog. She loves to go for hikes. You usually take a water bottle when you go hiking. It fits in a holder that you wear around your waist. When your dog gets thirsty, you share your water by pouring some into your hand and letting her lap it up. But this weekend you're planning a really long hike. You're going to need all the water in your bottle for yourself. That means you've got to take extra water along for your dog.

You don't want to take a backpack. So how are you going to carry another water bottle? Wait a minute . . . maybe your dog could carry one of her own? Can you invent something that will solve your problem?

Find a Solution!

Work with a small group to invent something to solve the problem. Use the steps below to guide your thinking.

1 Identify the Need
2 Brainstorm Solutions

Be creative with your brainstorming to invent a solution for this problem.

Science Notebook

Fun Facts

• Great white sharks are some of the largest predators in the ocean. The record for the longest great white ever caught is 5.9 meters (19.5 feet).

• In 1992, a Juan Fernandez fur seal became the first marine mammal to wear Crittercam. These rare seals live around Selkirk Island, about 965 kilometers (600 miles) off the coast of Chile in South America.

• Crittercam has revealed that green sea turtles groom themselves underwater. They can spend hours swimming along the ocean bottom, rubbing their heads, flippers, and shells against sponges, rocks, and corals.

Web Connection

For more information about Crittercam and the latest research being done with it, check out www.nationalgeographic.com/crittercam. You can also go to www.nationalgeographic.com and type "crittercam" in the search box. This will link you to additional articles about Crittercam and more behind-the-scenes information about the team and its expeditions.

Become an Armchair Explorer

You can also see Crittercam in action by watching videos that Greg Marshall's team has made with the help of the National Geographic Society. Look for these titles at your school or public library:

Great White Shark, 1994

Sea Monsters: Search for the Giant Squid, 1998

Diving with Seals, 1998

It takes more than one person to attach the small Crittercam to a large seal!

Glossary

buoyant tends to float

drag force that slows down an object moving through liquid or air

endangered at risk of dying out, or becoming extinct

groom to make clean or remove unwanted material

habitat place where something lives

harnesses straps for holding Crittercam onto an animal

molt to shed an outer layer, such as fur

prototype original model of something, on which later versions are based

remora fish with a suction-cup-like structure on its head that attaches itself to larger fish

streamlined shaped so that liquid or air flows easily around it

tether rope or line used to attach one object to another

Index